Disclaimer

Acknowledgements

I would like to acknowledge my husband Alan for his continued support and encouragement of all my work including this book.

I would also like to thank all my family and friends for their continued love and support through the good times and the not so good I have endured in my life. I am blessed and grateful to have you in my life. I love you all.

Dedication

I would like to dedicate this book to my beautiful daughter Niamh. I hope one day you will be able to find help and guidance though the principles in this book.

Table of Contents

Introduction

This aim of this book is to help the reader learn and remember how powerful our minds are in contributing to our overall physical and mental health and well-being. It is estimated that we think between 60,000 to 80,000 thoughts every day. Most of the thoughts we think are similar to the day before and the day before that. They become habitual and are not always helpful. We think a thought and this thought carries an emotion and this emotion will dictate how we behave in that particular moment. If we are thinking an angry thought we will feel the effect in our bodies as our jaw may clench, our muscles become tense and our heart beats faster. We might lash out verbally at the person we are angry toward and maybe later regret our hurtful words. Words are powerful. Words have consequences. We may forgive others or we may ask forgiveness for the hurtful words we say to another in the heat of the moment. These may be forgiven but not necessarily forgotten. We need to be conscious about the words we use.

We manifest all our experiences first through the power of thought and the meaning and emotion we give to our thoughts. Life is not about what happens, it's about the meaning we assign to the event or situation. If we harness the power within us to change how we feel in any given circumstance, we can change our perception of life events. The teachings in this book come from many great teachers and different traditions. Ultimately this book will hopefully inspire and empower you to take charge of your thinking in order to manifest good in our life and in the lives of others.

My story

I had been teaching a series of short classes in the field of self-development for several years to various groups in society, mainly to those suffering depression and other forms of mental illness. Whilst I was teaching all this 'good stuff' I too felt very positive about myself and life in general. I enjoyed this time of teaching as I also benefited and was able to apply the methodologies into my own life.

However once the six or eight week course had finished, I began to slip back into old patterns and ways of thinking. My life around the age of 40 began to fall apart. I was in self-destruct mode and this affected my relationships. I didn't feel good about myself and felt guilty because I felt I was a hypocrite as I was not always walking the talk so to speak. Even though I was very good at teaching others self-improvement tools and techniques I often failed to do the work on myself as much as I could have.

I do understand that when people's lives are not

working for them, and mine was not at the time it can be difficult to change your thinking.

I now know I have a choice in how I react to any given situation or person. I now know that I can allow another person to make me feel bad about myself only if I sanction it and give credence to it. I had previously allowed another person to treat me badly and disrespect me, but was at the same time learning to be more assertive. We teach people how to treat us.
I still was not accomplished at conflict management and this was reflected in my marriage.

On March 1, 2009 I started to make real positive changes in my life. I started to exercise for the first time in nearly 6 years. I began to meditate and use daily visualization techniques along with affirmations to clear the psoriasis. I tried not to refer to it as 'my' psoriasis as I did not want to feel I owned it but rather it was a condition my body was experiencing. I had

had psoriasis for over 20 years and it had spread in a

matter of a few months to my arms, neck and face.

This really concerned me as it was very

uncomfortable, itchy all the time causing me to

scratch 24/7 and visually unpleasant. Because I felt it

was unsightly looking, I allowed the psoriasis to

dictate what clothes I could and couldn't wear. I could

only wear cotton fabrics next to my skin as anything

else irritated it. I was very upset at the rate it was

spreading to new areas of my body and knew that my

negative thought patterns such as anger and

resentment had played a part in the spread of

psoriasis.

The skin represents boundaries. My skin was on fire

and very angry looking. I too felt my boundaries had

been breached and the outward appearance of my

skin reflected the fire within me because of this

breach.

I did not want to revert back to using steroid creams

as I had done previously, finding they thin the skin and almost as soon as I finished using the cream the psoriasis would come back with a vengeance.

I was well-read and qualified in various healing modalities and knew I had the power to heal myself using mind and body together. Using affirmations and visualization techniques to restore my body to its natural state of health would be one component. However, my thinking was off track and causing the spread of this condition and it was up to me and me alone to change.

Within a few days of really working at my positive affirmations for health the psoriasis on my face and neck disappeared. The patch on my left arm disappeared and my right arm was definitely more calm and less angry now.

In a strange sort of way, I have to be grateful to the psoriasis as it has brought to my attention exactly how off track my thinking had become. I felt quite liberated and powerful that I had the power to change the state of my health simply through my mental attitude and positive thinking. I now had a perfect opportunity to put into practice all my teachings. This was the beginning of my spiritual journey of healing and the beginning of my own metamorphosis.

Chapter One

There's power in our thoughts!

"Thoughts have power; thoughts are energy. And you can make your world or break it by your thinking."

Susan Taylor

I have had many examples in my life where I have been shown that what we think about is what we attract back into our life. We attract what we focus on or place our intention on. In other words, what we give our attention to expands. An example of this happened when I had been talking to a girlfriend of mine in Norwich, (a city in the east of England where I lived) one morning about a friendship I had lost because of a major disagreement between my husband and this friends husband. That afternoon I took my daughter to gymnastic class and to my great surprise this friend who I had fallen out with was there with her daughter. This was not the usual day for her daughter to attend gymnastics but because of snow earlier in the week her class had been rescheduled. I had not bumped into this friend for months following the disagreement but because I was talking about her that morning I felt I had attracted this scenario because it was the dominant thought in my consciousness at the time.

That same day I attended an incredible seminar given by Dr. David Hamilton at the Assembly Rooms in Norwich where he talked about his book, 'Law of Attraction'. He talked about how we could use our mind to heal our body by using visualization and affirmations.

I decided to put this idea to the test on the psoriasis I was suffering with for over 20 years. After 3 days of practicing affirmations and visualizing that my skin was completely clear and psoriasis free, I noticed the skin was less red in the patch I had on my inner elbow. I was impressed and although I had been teaching this kind of idea to various organizations and groups for several years I hadn't really given myself time to do the work on myself until now. This was a turning point for me and I really started to concentrate and give time to focus on my own healing.

These are the affirmations I repeated to myself:

My skin is soft, clear and smooth

My body is healthy and vibrant

I am filled with an abundance of energy

The healing process has begun

My body heals itself quickly and easily

Will Bowen, the author of the book 'A Complaint Free World' was also mentioned at the seminar I attended and so I bought and read the book.

At this time, I ordered my 'complaint free' purple bracelet and started wearing it. The idea behind the bracelet is that, every time you make a complaint, negative judgement, comment or criticism about another person or situation you must change the bracelet to the other hand. I amazed myself at how difficult it was to get through one whole day without changing the bracelet many times. Scientists say it takes 21 days to form a new habit so the challenge is to complete 21 consecutive days without complaining. Every time you slip up and complain you go right back to day 1. I am still working on the challenge! Complaining can be habitual. Wearing the bracelet was a great reminder to think before complaining or judging and it certainly did make me more aware of some bad habits of mine!!

I realize awareness is key to being able to successfully make any change in our life and of course these changes have to take place on a mental level first. In order to change our negative thought patterns, we must first be aware of the thoughts that are no longer productive to our wellbeing and mental health. The Brahma Kumaris say this, "Before you speak let your words pass through three gates: Is it true? Is it necessary? Is it kind?" This not only refers to the words we say to others and they to us, but also the words we say to ourselves! More on that topic later.

"Be the change you wish to see in the world"
Gandhi

Chapter Two

Mind / body connection

"The mind and the body are like parallel universes.

Anything that happens in the mental universe must

leave tracks in the physical one."

Deepak Chopra

Psychoneuroimmunology or PNI is the name for the

study of the mind-body connection. The idea being

that the mind and body are not separate entities. The

ancient philosopher Hippocrates stated that "The

natural healing force within each of us is the greatest

force in getting well." At the time Western medicine

did not agree that the mind and body were

interconnected and instead focused on treating

physical symptoms with drugs or surgery.

However, since the 1960's researchers have realized

that the mind does affect the healing process within

the body. Western style allopathic medicine is now

embracing the power of visualization, guided imagery and alternative healing methods such as yoga and meditation.

Medical doctors such as Bernie Siegel and Carl Simonton have both been using guided imagery for over 20 years in the treatment of cancer.

Freud believed the unconscious mind made up 90% of the mind and the conscious mind only 10%.

We are all aware that stress makes people more susceptible to illness by lowering immunity.

The meaning we attach to things is extremely important in determining how we feel.

We know that our emotions are strongly linked to our body cells. When we feel embarrassed the blood rushes to our face and we turn red. When we hear something that frightens us the hairs on our arms may stand up and our heart will begin to beat faster. If we feel nervous or excited our palms may begin to sweat. When we watch a sad movie, this can activate tears. My husband thinks I am emotionally incontinent when it comes to watching sad movies! I cried while watching Heidi with my then 9 year old daughter!

A study published in 2002 by researchers at the Carnegie Mellon University Dept. of Psychology found that people with positive emotions were less likely to catch the common cold. A study by the University of California at San Francisco, also published in 2002, reported that people with AIDS who had a positive attitude had a lower death rate from AIDS-related complications.

Our thoughts attract thoughts, if you focus on what you don't want, that is exactly what you will attract. So, as the Chinese proverb states "be careful what you wish for". Happy people focus on positive aspects of life and attract positive outcomes.

The mind uses the body to express itself. We need to understand the link and what it is that is being communicated through the body. By understanding this communication, we can begin our own inner healing.

In order to find the psychological and emotional causes of our mind/body expression we usually need to look back 6-12 months prior to the onset of the physical problem. Ask yourself the question, "What was going on in my life then". Was work or my personal life difficult or stressful?

I love this expression, 'energy flows where attention goes'. What you focus on expands, what you resist persists.

A large number of physical ailments and diseases have an emotional cause. If emotional pain and trauma are not released, or feelings are being suppressed they can manifest as physical illness. Healing the disease or condition can mean healing the emotion with which it is associated. This may involve us letting go of guilt, criticism, fear and resentment.

It is true that the mind uses the body as a last resort to give us a message that there is an imbalance and it is here we need to direct our attention and focus our awareness. We need to be deeply honest with ourselves and acknowledge our true feelings about a situation that is current or in the past. The body may also be manifesting an inner problem that has already been resolved. I can acknowledge that the psoriasis I had on my legs in September 2009 had been aggravated by a deeply emotional period with a close family member.

I had to admit to my feelings of intense resentment and anger and then release and let go. I realized I was the one who was hurting by clinging onto these negative feelings and that the person involved had moved on and was not in the slightest bit bothered. I still to this day have to work on myself and do affirmations and visualization work as well as work on forgiveness. I am given many different opportunities almost on a daily basis where I need to examine my triggers, my emotional responses and question my reactions to people, situations and life events. I guess I'll be on this spiritual journey till I check out and that's okay with me!

I feel blessed that I have many tools to utilize in order for me to maintain good health both physically and emotionally. During this difficult period business was slow and it therefore allowed me time to work on myself and confront issues about myself and grow from inner work. I can look back now and see that this was all happening at the right time for me. Every cloud has a silver lining!

I had to ask myself some difficult questions such as, 'What is the nature or function of the part of my body affected by the condition?
'What are my inner thoughts, feelings and language I

use to describe the condition?

'What was going on in my life around the onset of the condition?

'What is the 'pay off ' I get by me keeping the condition?

On a metaphysical level each of our individual body parts represents a deeper spiritual meaning. The body stores all our past emotions, traumas and memories. These are stored in the body as energy and can manifest itself in a variety of ailments and diseases.

Other body parts!

Eyes.

They say the eyes are the 'windows to the soul'. Our eyes communicate our feelings towards others and how we see the world. Our ability or inability to accept what we are seeing is also reflected in the health of our eyes. Our tears are a release of emotions, a reflection of our inner pain or indeed joy. The left eye represents the inner, emotional and intuitive part of us. The right eye represents more aggressive and assertive energies.

Ears.

Our ears are a vehicle for hearing things. People who are not happy with what they are hearing close off the energy to the ears and this can manifest itself in all sorts of problems relating to the ears. Loss of hearing or earache can occur from being over criticized either by oneself or others. The ears are also used to find balance and equilibrium. If our ears are out of balance this could also be true about aspects of our life! Worth thinking about the next time we have ear problems!

Nose.

The main function of the nose is to help us breathe. The breath represents life. Whenever we have blockages in the nose we are on a subconscious level trying to shut down the breathing or 'living' mechanism. Catching a cold is often synonymous with needing time to reconnect with our inner self and our desire to live. The sinuses are the passages of air that are connected to thought, to communication and our awareness. Blocked sinuses relate to mental blockages where we are unable to communicate.

I have had sinus issues all my life including two operations and I can also see where for most of my life I have been unable to communicate my truth to certain people close to me for fear of not been accepted. This does not help me show my authentic self which does not honor who I really am.

Grinding teeth.

We grind our teeth with anger, usually an anger that is not being expressed. Again I can relate to a time where I used to grind my teeth in my sleep and the link to my inability to express my anger in a healthy way.

Neck.

The neck is the bridge between the head and the heart. A stiff neck may mean we are becoming rigid in our ideas, not seeing all sides of the story so to speak, becoming narrow minded. Through the neck we manifest thoughts and ideas into action. Our inner feelings from the heart can be expressed. Difficulty in the throat is associated with resistance to accepting our reality. We often hear the expressions 'eat your words' meaning swallow your feelings. 'I can't swallow that' or "I find that hard to swallow' means we are finding it hard to accept that idea.

Heart.

The heart is associated with the thymus gland and the production of T-cells in the immune system. When we have positive and loving feelings and thoughts our immune system is stronger and better able to fight infection and disease. On the other hand, when we experience negative emotions such as anger, hatred, resentment our thymus and immune system is weakened and we become more susceptible to illness.

'Letting go' of our suffering is the hardest but most rewarding work we can ever do. It is however for most people one of the most difficult things to do. If we can view this 'letting go' as a reward to ourselves in terms of freeing us from suffering the process can be easier.

The healing process begins when we are able to accept and love ourselves as we truly are 'warts and all' and being able to love ourselves whilst making the changes we need to make. By using visualization, meditation, prayer and body work the process of change and transformation will become easier. We may also need to ask ourselves the question, "what is stopping me from allowing myself to heal and become whole?"

We are all on our own personal journey and there is no one path. Each of us has to find our own path, a way that works best for us. There will always be signposts to help us on the right path we just have to be aware and act on them. Trust your inner guidance. Think of it in terms of your inner GPS, if we go off on the wrong road we will be redirected until we are on the correct one. Learn from your mistakes. Insanity can be described as doing the same thing over and over and expecting different results! I have certainly been guilty of this at times in my life!

Our future depends on our present thoughts, feelings and attitudes. I have found that it is truly empowering to know that thoughts are just thoughts and thoughts can be changed. We choose what we think so if we have flaws in our thinking we have the power to change that, the choice is ours. We have a choice in how we think and react to every situation, good or bad. The choice we make will have an impact on our lives.

Developing compassion, forgiveness, gentleness and awareness in our self and towards others is the first step towards healing. We have to be ready to look within and that is not an easy thing to do because it requires looking at the parts of our personality that we do not like that much.

Sometimes our body creates the disease. Disease, a word that can be divided in two to read, "dis" "ease" can often make us have a "wake-up" call and take a look at our beliefs, attitudes and emotions. Our external body is a reflection of our internal mind. Disease within the body can be a real motivation for us to make necessary changes be they on a physical, emotional or spiritual level. The answers are always within us if we only are willing to take a look. It might not be as scary as we think! We need to make peace with ourselves first and be gentle as we begin this process.

I believe that most diseases have an underlying emotional basis. Disease and illness are signs that the body uses to show us where we are not loving. Ultimately we get ill to teach us love. It is a gift, although this might be difficult to understand when you are living with the pain and discomfort of being ill.

According to Dr. Gabor Maté, author of the book 'When the Body Says No', when people can't say No the body says it for them in the form of illness. I find the idea of there being a link between psychology and physiology totally fascinating and it makes complete sense to me. Dr. Maté says that women are the stress absorbers of the environment including the stress of their men. That's why married men live longer than unmarried men and unmarried women live longer than married women!

The suppression of healthy anger is linked to the development of disease and the expression of unhealthy anger is linked to disease. People who suppress their anger suppress their immune system. The body and mind cannot be separated.

He goes on to say that human beings have two main needs on an emotional level, attachment and authenticity.

If we suppress our healthy anger, we will suppress both our emotional system and nervous system as both are connected. When we don't protect our boundaries the immune system becomes confused and this leads to autoimmune diseases such as eczema and psoriasis where the immune system attacks the body. This is what happens to people who emotionally suppress themselves. The disease we experience can be a blessing if it brings us back to our authentic selves.

When symptoms come along, headache, rash, digestive issues, sinus pain, colds or even more serious conditions we need to ask the questions,

'what is my body saying no to that I'm not'? 'Where

do I need to be more authentic?' We need to reflect

on who we are and what we need to do to be our

authentic self.

Chapter Three

How can I forgive the past?

"To forgive is to set a prisoner free and discover the

prisoner was you."

Lewis B. Swedes

We can often gain insights from the past as to why we are the way we are today, but when we dwell too much in the past and keep reliving our hurts, this only serves us to remain 'stuck' in the past and that is truly not a good way to live as it will never allow us to be happy.

It makes more sense to learn from the past but not live there. We must learn to forgive the past otherwise we will continue to hold onto the past which perpetuates our suffering and leaves us feeling like the victim.

Forgiveness does not come easy to many of us. We feel we are letting the person who has hurt us 'off the hook' so to speak. Forgiveness does not mean we condone the poor behavior or actions of another or saying that it doesn't matter. Forgiveness is not about that other person; it is about you. It is about telling yourself you are not going to carry this hurt around any longer and let it upset and ruin your day, or your life. You are freeing your mind and deciding to 'let it go' in order to have peace in your heart again.

You may like to try writing a letter along these lines. You may consider burning it when written and releasing all the feelings attached to it.

Dear (blank) I hold you in my heart with love and compassion. I forgive you for the painful choices and mistakes you have made in the past. I now release and let go of the feelings I have towards the experience, with love.

"We must develop and maintain the capacity to

forgive. He who is devoid of the power to forgive is devoid of the power to love. There is some good in the worst of us and some evil in the best of us. When we discover this, we are less prone to hate our enemies."

Martin Luther King Jr.

Affirmations to help with forgiveness:

I now forgive you and release you

My heart is open to receive love in my life

I release you and let you go

I forgive myself and am ready and willing to move on

Chapter Four

Metamorphic Technique

"Metamorphosis is the movement of transformation from who you are to what you can be, freeing your creativity."

Gaston Saint Pierre

Founder of the Metamorphic Technique

What is it?

We get a sense of the Metamorphic Technique by looking at how life expresses itself in nature. A little acorn can grow into a big oak tree or a caterpillar into a butterfly. What happens inside the cocoon of a caterpillar? The form of the caterpillar dissolves into a jelly-like substance which eventually gives rise to a new form, being a butterfly. In other words, life simply expresses itself in a different form. However, as well as transformation expressing itself at the physical level, there is also the potential for it to occur at the emotional or consciousness level. In other words, a 'change of mind' can also naturally occur whereby we suddenly find ourselves in a much more fulfilling relationship with our life and the world at large.

What happens in a Metamorphic Technique session? The practitioner uses a light touch on the feet, hands and head, while at the same time, paying attention to not impose their beliefs or limited understanding on the person receiving the session. In this regard, the founder, Gaston Saint-Pierre, defines the Metamorphic Technique as simply being a practice of detachment, which means providing the person receiving the session with an environment free from direction, interference and preconceived ideas. The practitioners have absolutely no expectations of there being any right or wrong way for people to feel or behave either during or after a session.

Benefits people report.
The Metamorphic Technique is suitable for everyone,

regardless of age, circumstance or condition of your life.

Practitioners make no claims for the Technique, but it is a fact that many people who have sessions have reported an array of different benefits. For example, a number of people have talked about improvements in their physical health. From a mental and emotional perspective people have reported letting go of past hurts and self-limiting beliefs. People also mention discovering strengths that they were not even aware they had.

From a social perspective people have reported an increasing ability to be more of who they truly are rather than how others think they should be.

History.

Gaston Saint-Pierre founded the Metamorphic Technique in the late 1970s. He had long held a passionate interest in the question of transformation. When he encountered the Prenatal Therapy work of

Robert St. John, this proved to be the final trigger to the emergence of the practice he named the Metamorphic Technique. He founded the Metamorphic Association in 1979 and it became a registered educational charity in 1984.

Metamorphosis is a Greek word. The Oxford English dictionary says it is 'a complete change in the appearance, circumstance, condition and character of a person'.
The word 'meta' means a transmutation into a higher substance'. Metamorphosis does not 'cure', it enables us to create a different attitude towards life, and it is this which alters our troubles, we cease to create illness.

The Metamorphic Technique is a wonderful contributor to the field of holistic health where change, transformation and healing are sought. With MT, instead of concentrating on symptoms or difficulties in the person's life, the practitioner acts as a catalyst, providing the person with a 'safe space', free of any judgement, direction, preconceived ideas or interference. It is this innate intelligence within each of us that can move his or her energy in a way that is right for them. This might be for example, a change in career, a change in life/work balance, new lifestyle habits.

Science now tells us that every cell in the human body is a hologram containing all the information and intelligence of every other cell and therefore of the whole body. The Metamorphic Technique (MT for short) works on the spinal reflexes of the foot, hand and head which correlate to the 38 weeks we were carried in our mothers' womb. This is the time all our characteristics, physical, behavioral, emotional and spiritual were established. During a MT session deeply rooted energy blockages may be loosened and released allowing energy to move more freely and allowing the person to become open to the possibility of positive transformation. This may mean letting go of old ways of being that no longer serve us.

On my journey of healing I discovered MT. I had been an exhibitor at a Mind/Body/Spirit exhibition in Norwich in 2009 and had a mini session whilst taking a short break. I thought it was quite relaxing but was not overly impressed with this gentle rubbing of my feet. I was a trained massage therapist and liked a firm touch not a light touch. However, something drew me to wanting to have a full session and so I had my first session with Tripuri Dunne on October 13, 2009. It is a gentle touch on the spinal reflexes of the feet, hands and head. When she was working on my feet five minutes into the session she began to yawn and yawn continuously. She didn't apologize for her yawning and I thought that a bit weird and if honest, somewhat unprofessional. I asked her if she was tired. She said, "no not at all". She told me I was releasing stuff especially in the area of the heart and it was being released through her in the form of yawning which is a release of energy.

During the session I had a lot of emotions come up for me about my childhood and upbringing and I realized I needed to forgive my parents for not being who or what I wanted them to be all the time. Now that I too am a mother I know our parents are always doing the best they can with the knowledge and understanding they have at the time and that too was true for my parents who loved us in their own way. Nobody is perfect and nobody has perfect parents, but we are all doing the best we can with the level of awareness we have at any given time.

I continued regular sessions of MT and worked through some big personal issues. I felt it helped me so much, that later that year I trained with Tripuri to qualify as a Metamorphic Technique practitioner.

Since the day I had my MT session I gave myself

time, or rather the universe gave me time, to do a lot of soul searching and reflection. I realized I had a lot of issues to work through and that I had not been the best version of myself that I could have been over the previous 2 years. I felt ready and stronger to make changes in my life and I wanted to be able to enjoy life to the full which was something I was not able to do previously.

The Metamorphic Technique allowed me to cope with some major changes that were about to unfold in my life.

I began reading 'Power of the Soul' by John Holland and it was the perfect book for me at that time.

John Holland's book was revolutionary for me. Thank you God for guiding me to find that book on the library shelf. I don't believe it was a coincidence. The mathematical term where two angles meet is to 'coincide' we then change the word to mean 'happenstance'! I am a firm believer that there are no coincidences as happenstance in life. Everything happens for a reason! The people we meet or circumstances we encounter have all been placed on our path so we can learn from and grow. They all play a role in our destiny and in making us who we are and what we become. Even the bad things that happen to us contain blessings if we take the time to examine them.

Chapter Five

Dare to dream?

"The biggest adventure you can take is to live the life

of your dreams"

Oprah Winfrey

To achieve our dreams, we need to be really specific about what we want. Never focus on what you do not want. Visualize the dream in minute detail. Ask yourself," what it will feel, sound, hear, smell like". I have used this technique when I have been preparing to be interviewed on radio, given speeches or encountering a daunting task. You have to believe it to see it, not the other way around! If you cannot visualize it, it won't happen.

The painter Vincent Van Gough was asked how he produced such beautiful work. He said, "I dream my painting, and then I paint my dream".

Ask yourself, 'How will I feel when I have achieved my

goal or dream?' You must see yourself achieving your goal and believe it to be possible for it ever to become a reality.

At that time in my life I felt I was preparing, or rather my soul was preparing, for something big! I was not sure exactly what or when but I could feel it. I was being guided in several ways.

Firstly, being able to attend Toastmasters to gain confidence in public speaking.

Secondly finding Metamorphic Technique brought to light the abuse I was doing to my mind and body at the time.

Prosperity Consciousness.

When we realize and focus on what we already have in our life the universe brings more good things to us. Similarly, the more you think you don't have what you want the further it goes from you. The power to transform your life is in your heart, we just need the courage to open our hearts to find the key. This is prosperity consciousness.

"We should love people and use money. Lack and limitation can only exist when we make room for them in our minds. But prosperity consciousness knows no lack and no limitation.", says Bob Proctor, one the authors of The Secret.

Affirmation:

   "I am prosperous, I am wealthy, money is good"

Remember the subconscious mind does not think. It merely accepts images and then moves them into form.

Napoleon Hill author of 'Think and Grow Rich' said "Whatever the mind can conceive and believe it can achieve". This is so very true.

The Buddha says, "We are not the victim, we are the creator of our own healing process and we determine how long it will take." This depends on how quickly we learn whatever lesson we need to learn. Our relationships with others are simply mirrors of our relationship with our self.

Trust yourself.

We should not be overly concerned about what others say or think about you. It's your life, be more concerned with what you say to yourself and how you treat you.

Guilt is a highly destructive emotion that eats away at us and robs our soul of joy. Trust that your soul knows what is best for you and listen when it gives you signs and signals which can come in many different forms. The soul wants you to be happy and fulfilled. To hear your soul, you need to slow down, connect and listen to its guidance. Remember, the difficult experiences of life are just as important in teaching us lessons as the good ones.

Chapter Six

Law of Vibration / Attraction

'What you think you become.

What you feel you attract.

What you imagine you create.'

Buddha

Everything is energy and everything vibrates. The acorn looks solid but in fact it is a mass of molecules vibrating at a very high speed. It has a nucleus at its center which dictates the vibratory rate. Likewise, our subconscious mind is the nucleus which determines what we will eventually grow into. It dictates the vibration you will be and also controls what you will attract to you and what you will repel.

The Law of Vibration is the basis of the Law of Attraction. The Law of Attraction will deliver to you all that you want and do not want and this depends on what you are focusing on and the vibration you are currently giving off. We often hear people talking about 'good vibes' or 'bad vibes' when referring to the vibration they are experiencing in terms of another person, place or situation.

We need to ask ourselves, 'What am I in harmonious vibration with at the moment'? This is largely linked to how we think and feel about a situation or person at any given time. We must remember that the Law of Attraction is always at work whether we believe so or not. It doesn't have rest days!

An example of the Law of Attraction working came about as I was asked to give a talk to the Women's Institute in Buxton, Norfolk. My sense of direction was never very good and I began to realize I had no clue where Buxton was. I relied heavily on our satellite navigation system for every new journey. My husband Alan was in Houston on business that week and had taken the portable satellite navigation (GPS) with him for use in the hire car. As I was doing my usual morning walk around the village and was thinking about how useful it would be to have the satellite navigation for the talk that night to be sure I would arrive on time without getting lost. No sooner than I'd had the thought when a friend of mine pulled up in her car and after I had asked her did she know where Buxton was, she said, "would you like to borrow my satellite navigation". This was a perfect example of the Law of Attraction at play. You attract what you think about most. So be careful what you think about!

The Law of Vibration and Attraction explains that everything vibrates constantly. Conscious awareness of vibration is called feelings. It is our thoughts that control our vibrations and this in turn dictates what we attract into our lives, good or bad.

'*See yourself living in abundance and you will attract it*'.

Rhonda Byrne

The power of our deliberate intention.

We must remember that we are vibrational beings living in a vibrational universe. We are continually giving and receiving vibrations. What we are thinking and the vibrations we offer are reflected in the Law of Attraction. It does not matter what wording we use for example, "I'm focusing, I'm imagining, I'm thinking, the Law of Attraction is responding. The more attention we give to a particular thought or feeling be it positive or negative it will become the dominant thought in your vibration offering to the universe. If we understand this, then we realize we are the creator of our own reality.

Have you ever been thinking about a person and then the phone rings and it is that person? This is the law of synchronicity. I had an example of this recently. I had been thinking about a client of mine who had come to me for a series of Metamorphic Technique sessions. She became pregnant after the third session of MT and was delighted as she and her husband had been trying for a while. The MT allowed her life force to be free to do what was right for her at the time and that was to fall pregnant. She had moved to Newfoundland 6 months later. She kept popping into my consciousness one morning and so I decided to email her to see how she was getting on and enquire had she had the baby. Her husband replied to me straight away to tell me she had given birth to a baby boy that morning!

Law of Reciprocity asks us to reciprocate only positive actions of deeds. When someone says something positive to you reciprocate it. However, it is not the same for a negative. When someone says something negative, step aside and let that negativity keep on going, don't be a part of it. This is easier said than done I know as it is human nature to sometimes want to become defensive or retaliate with equal negativity. I try and take the view that if someone is unduly rude, hurtful or critical of you it is they who are in a bad place and you must not allow yourself to take on

board their 'stuff'. People who are in a 'good place'

mentally and emotionally do not hurt others. Hurt

people, hurt people!

The most famous quote by Lao Tzu, author of the Tao Te Ching is, "A journey of a thousand miles begins with a single step". These are powerful words of wisdom.

I was drawn to the quote on 'living without sickness' in the 71st verse which states

"Knowing ignorance is strength

ignoring knowledge is sickness

only when we are sick of our sickness

shall we cease to be sick.

The sage is not sick

but is sick of sickness

this is the secret of health."

An ancient proverb says that if a man has a happy mind, he will have a happy body. A happy mind is sick of sickness. So we need to free ourselves from sickness by using our mind to attract health.

Chapter Seven

Confidence

"Because one believes in oneself one doesn't try to convince others. Because one is content with oneself one doesn't need others' approval. Because one accepts oneself, the whole world accepts him or her."

Lao Tzu

Old patterns of thinking keep you stuck in habits and patterns that no longer serve our higher self. As Einstein said, the definition of insanity is to keep on doing the same things over and over again and expecting a different result! What you practice you become. To high achievers and successful people failure doesn't mean it is time to give up, it merely means let's take a step back, take stock of what went wrong and why, then learn from the mistake and move forward. If you can do this, you will be more prepared for success the next time.

Ask yourself the question, 'who would you be and how would you look, and act if you were already naturally confident right now?"

Confidence is about an attitude to life that leads to success and is driven by motivation.

Aristotle said, "We are what we repeatedly do. Excellence then is not an act, but a habit."

Confident people give out more positive energy and so by the Law of Attraction attract like-minded confident people. Gaining confidence is about being able to access one's inner resources and putting ideas into action.

The EGO, sometimes known in more spiritual language to mean 'edging God out', has two roles. Firstly, to look good and secondly to be right. To find the authentic self or the real you we have to peel back the layers just like an onion. The authentic self is naturally confident and completely unique. You are one of a kind and we should acknowledge and rejoice in this fact.

George Bernard Shaw said, "those who cannot change their minds cannot change anything."
All personal transformation starts in the mind.
We have two minds, the conscious mind and the subconscious or unconscious mind. The conscious mind is the mind that has the continual internal dialogue going on all day long. It's what we come to think of as 'me'. It is however very limited and can only hold together a limited number of ideas at any given time. The majority of our life is run by the unconscious mind.

As mentioned in Chapter 2, the unconscious mind is a much larger mind and can process millions of messages of sensory information every second. It holds all your memories, intelligence and wisdom. It also is responsible for all our automatic behavior that we use in our life. Learning to tie our shoe laces was once controlled by the conscious mind as we needed to focus and concentrate a lot whilst learning the skill but after it is mastered it becomes controlled by the unconscious mind and we can direct our hands to tie our shoe laces and have a conversation at the same time. This frees up the conscious mind to do other jobs.

John Dryden said, "we first make our habits, then our habits make us."

Our unconscious mind allows us to do habitual activities without having to think too much about them, washing our face, cleaning teeth, brushing hair, eating driving etc.

It also controls the sympathetic nervous system making our heart beat, releasing hormones and a whole host of automatic responses within our body. The brain is a mass of neural pathways and every action we take creates new connections.

Each time we repeat an action, that specific neural pathway is strengthened, just like a muscle becomes stronger the more time it is used. This is how a new

habit is formed. In order for a new habit to be

accepted we need to rehearse over and over again in

our mind visualizing us performing the new habit.

This will guarantee success. In terms of increasing

confidence, the more you practice thinking about your

confidence you are sending signals to the

unconscious mind to behave as a naturally confident

person.

Tips for Building Confidence

Strengthen your mind

Knowledge facilitates richer experiences and opportunities. Push your limits and find out where your true ability lies. The mind knows where you are and can take you to where it wants to go.

Fear less and dare more often!

Do at least one thing every day that scares you. Step outside your comfort zone even if it is something small. Don't let fear paralyze you. All we need to do is overcome our fears and dare to follow our dreams. New experiences make our life richer.

Have a purpose in Life

Purpose gives meaning to our life. It changes our attitude towards to life. Find out what excites and motivates you.

Let go of small stuff.

What you are putting up with stops us from being ourselves. Try not to over-react, blow things out of proportion, hold on too tightly or focus on the negative aspects of life.

Prevent the little things in life from immobilizing you, and weighing you down.

Be fully present.

To be fully present is to have no preoccupations with past or future. Remain in the now even when focusing on the past or speculating on the future.

Savor every moment and appreciate the beauty in life.

Set goals and commit to action.

Decide right now that it is important to live a life of no regrets and then set goals to support your purpose and dreams.

Goals help us focus on what it is we want and move in a chosen direction.

Spend time each day with confident people.

Their energy will be infectious and their inner strength will be empowering.

Find a mentor.

Someone you look up to and can learn from.

List reasons why you should be confident.

Past successes, skills / qualities / past achievements

Preparation makes perfect.

Practice your skills until you are confident.

Compare your progress with previous results.

Learn from the successes of others. Do not compare yourself to them.

Make a public declaration.

Tell someone that you are going to succeed at (blank) You'll demand more of yourself and be accountable.

Affirmations for

Self-Esteem and Self- Confidence

I am totally adequate for all situations

I choose to feel good about myself. I am worthy of my own love.

I stand on my own two feet. I accept and use my own power.

It is safe for me to speak up for myself.

It does not matter what other people say or do. What matters is how I choose to react to believe about myself.

I take a deep breath and allow myself to relax. My entire body calms down.

I am loved and accepted exactly as I am, right here and right now.

I see the world through eyes of love and acceptance. All is well in my world.

My self-esteem is high because I honor who I am.

I accept others as they are; and they, in turn, accept me.

I am wonderful, and I feel great. I am grateful for my life.

This is the only time I get to live today. I choose to enjoy it.

I have the self-esteem, power, and confidence to move forward in life with ease.

The greatest gift I can give myself is unconditional love.

I love myself exactly as I am. I no longer wait to be perfect in order to love myself.

I am a confident and capable woman / man.

Chapter Eight

Self-talk

"You've been criticizing yourself for years and it hasn't worked. Try approving of yourself and see what happens."

Louise Hay

Our self-talk will do one of two things. It will empower us or defeat and destroy us. How is yourself-talk affecting you and the decisions you make in life? Most people are continuously feeding their unconscious mind with negative thoughts, criticizing themselves and then wonder why they feel bad! That negative voice in your head is affecting, in a detrimental way every aspect of your life. You need to change the way you speak to yourself in order to see positive results.

"Whether you think you can or think you can't you're right"

Henry Ford

New research has shown that consistent patterns of thinking and behavior actually lead to physical changes in the shape of the brain which would suggest that it is worth repeating the' perfect scenario' in your mind many times in order to see and experience the benefits.

Visualization skills are used by top athletes. I was fortunate to have seen Usain Bolt, the fastest man on the planet, win the 100metre sprint at the 2012 London Olympics. You can be guaranteed Bolt utilizes visualization techniques as part of his mental training, seeing himself sprinting faster than his competitors, always coming first over the finishing line.

I have also had the privilege to coach many elite triathletes in Houston, Texas over the last ten years helping them achieve their physical goals through using mind power techniques to help overcome any mental obstacles that could stand in the way of them performing to the best of their ability and achieving their goals. Although it is super important for these athletes to be physically prepared for their events they also need practice in mental strength techniques so they can endure the hardship and not give up. I have had incredible success with these amazing athletes and they have been a wonderful example of how powerful and important it is to use our mind to achieve our goals. All dreams begin in our mind and come to fruition through our thoughts as well of a heck of a lot of hard work!

Emotional intelligence.

Our emotions are important signals to us. They are our unconscious mind telling us that there is something going on in our life that we need to pay attention to. It is important to be aware of our emotions as they are there to be listened to and not suppressed. If we do not acknowledge our feelings, they can erupt at a later stage and can lead to depression and illness within our body.

Our self-belief whether it be positive or negative will become a self-fulfilling prophecy. We can use this to our advantage if we become more aware of our internal dialogue and change our thinking patterns from negative to positive. Awareness is the first step to changing our thoughts.

Cognitive dissonance is the state of holding two conflicting or inconsistent ideas, beliefs or opinions at the same time. It is so uncomfortable to cope with this that people will unconsciously seek to reduce this inner conflict by changing one or both of these ideas so that they fit better together.

If you want to be confident and successful but another part of you doesn't believe this is a real possibility then you will self-sabotage an event, situation or opportunity that could have brought you greater confidence or success. We need to be in alignment with what we want and our belief that it is possible in order to create a successful outcome.

Staying power.

Joanna was a single mum living on a social security allowance of seventy English pounds a week. She had an idea for a children's book and spent her time in cafes working on her book. When she submitted it for publication it was rejected by every major publishing company in the UK. Publishers thought it was too long a book for children to read.

Finally, one publisher decided to take a chance on publishing her book. Today 'Harry Potter' is one of the greatest children's books ever written and J.K. Rowling is a very wealthy lady. She had staying power and refused to take no for an answer. She showed perseverance and self-belief.

A belief is only a repetitive thought that you have been thinking. It has become your dominant thought and you believe it whether it be the truth or not. When we focus on a particular thought the universe will give us

a physical manifestation of whatever it is we have

been thinking, good or bad. It is said that about 90%

of every creation is completed before we get to see

any real physical evidence of manifestation. Life for

all of us is full of potential manifestations as a direct

result of the thoughts we have been thinking. Some

of these manifestations we will be happy about and

some we will definitely not. When we become aware

beings we can choose to turn our thoughts in the

direction of the things we want to experience. We can

deactivate our negative vibration when we realize we

are attracting unwanted experiences in our life and we

do this through our thoughts.

Our emotional health is an excellent indicator of whether our thoughts are helpful to us or not. Ask yourself, 'how am I feeling right now about a particular person or situation you are encountering?' So, as you go through your day try and become aware of your thoughts and emotions knowing that you are creating your own reality and also that if our thoughts are not on a vibrational frequency that is for our higher good that we have the power to change this.

No matter how the emotions feel, good or bad be proud and pleased with yourself for being aware of them. Acknowledge that your emotions are a vibrational indicator pointing out to you your current alignment with your source. Nothing is more important than that I feel good. The better I feel, the more I am allowing all the wonderful life experiences to flow into my life.

Deciding to be happy!

The key to being a happy person is making the decision to be happy. All sounds very simple you might say, but it is true. Our ego does battle with our desire to be happy but happiness comes from within. It is not something someone can give us. Our human condition always gives us choice. We choose how we see things; do we see the glass as half empty or half full?

Ghandi said, "Happiness is when what you think, what you say and what you do are in harmony."

I listened to an interesting radio program about a couple who wanted to be married but not referred to as married but instead be called 'civil partners'. During the marriage vows couples pledge to love each other for 'richer, poorer, sickness and in health, for better and worse'. The real purpose of marriage is to teach the couple how to truly love themselves, the parts they both like and dislike about themselves.

Understanding the purpose of marriage can free couples from the painful myth that their partner is there to make them happy. Love is not a static thing, it is constantly changing and growing.

The quality of our life depends on the quality of our relationships. Stating the obvious, we know women and men are different. In general women talk more than men. Women speak on average 20,000 words a day in comparison to men at 7,000. Men are inclined to use the left side of the brain associated with logic, and are interested in facts and figures. Women find fulfillment in relationships and do things so as to be together whereas men get together to do things. We all have different filters and see things differently. Unconditional love begins with our self. When we love ourselves it is only then we can really love others. When we can be unconditional in our love our relationships will be transformed.

Practice the affirmation:

'I love and accept myself exactly where I am.'

This allows us to be open to the possibility of change.

We have the choice to focus on what is wrong with our life or what is going right for us. Remember the universe will give us more of what we focus on. If we have thoughts of lack, we get more of lack. Think thoughts of abundance and we get more. Ask yourself the question, 'do I believe I deserve to be happy? It is our right to be happy. When we are happy we have a responsibility to share happiness and joy with others.

Negative Influences on Confidence Levels

We are all born with a degree of natural confidence.

However, our natural confidence is affected by

negative influences. Criticism destroys confidence.

Blame and Criticism

Ask yourself the questions:

'Who did you receive criticism from, parents, teachers,

bosses, spouse or partners?'

'How did the criticism affect you?

Write down your answers.

Blame and criticism can make us think that everything

that goes wrong is our fault. A child or indeed an

adult who is criticized will become highly sensitive to

criticism and will blame themselves when things don't

work out. They will often stop taking risks for fear of

failure.

Positive feedback or constructive criticism is very

different from being criticized. They will have two

different outcomes. Giving constructive feedback is a skill in itself. If done properly the self-esteem of the received will remain intact and the person will feel good about themselves but know there are things that can be improved on the next time. It is a general rule of thumb when giving constructive feedback, to point out the good parts of for example a task well done and then look at how the task could be improved upon. Feedback given in a critical manner with a harsh tone of voice can destroy the self-esteem of that person and leave long term damage if it is being done on a regular basis.

Conformity.

Have you ever been in a room full of people and knew the answer to a question asked but stayed quiet in case you were wrong? This is probably because the last time you spoke out you were laughed at for being wrong or teased because you were always right. You decide to conform with others and end up not being true to yourself. This can lead to great remorse and a lack of self-confidence. It takes courage to stand up and be heard even if others may disagree of laugh behind your back.

Exclusion.

Being excluded from a group can have a powerfully damaging effect on your confidence. It creates a feeling of isolation and loneliness and a feeling that you are not good enough, there must be something wrong with you. Think back to your childhood days. When were you excluded from joining in? How did this make you feel?

Competition.

We are introduced to the idea of competition from an early age, for example, school sports, exams. We are compared to the successes of others. If you compete and don't win on a regular basis you may begin to feel you are no good. You may develop an attitude of,

'What's the point in trying'. If you at first don't succeed try, try again. We can learn from our mistakes be they large or little and be able to improve the next time. Never give up!

Disappointment.

We experience disappointments in many different areas of our life. For example, maybe you were due for promotion and then get overlooked with no explanation. Maybe someone hurt and disappointed you in a relationship. You become wary of commitment in case you get let down. We start to mistrust people and our confidence levels plummet. Promises + disappointment = mistrust.

Perfectionism.

This often stems from our childhood where parents for example have very high expectations of us.
You end up thinking failure is unacceptable.
You don't let other people see your mistakes.

You anticipate and fear disapproval.

You constantly seek reassurance.

You criticize yourself for not being perfect.

We put tremendous pressure upon ourselves to be perfect all the time.

Dominance.

Bullying or being undermined in front of others can have a devastating effect on self-confidence and can lead to:

You taking on the victim role and accepting the blame for everything.

You give too much of yourself to others, you feel that is expected.

You find it hard to say 'NO'.

You don't value yourself and attribute great importance to others.

You let people 'walk all over you'.

Chapter Nine

Think yourself out of depression

"No storm, not even the ones in your life can last

forever. The storm is just passing over."

Iyanla Vanzant

Reprinted in full is an article I wrote for the Eastern

Daily Press and Evening News, published February

10, 2009, '*Think Yourself Out of Depression*'

Start of article:

"Rethink, a leading mental health charity launched a
successful campaign in Norwich during 2006 to stamp out
the stigma attached to people with mental health problems.
Norwich, UK was chosen as the first site for an anti-stigma
pilot in March 2006. Levels of mental health problems in
Norwich are high. More anti-depressants are prescribed in
Norwich than anywhere else in Central or Eastern
England. Norwich traditionally has
had a higher suicide rate than the national average and
has the "unenviable position as a center of high rates of
self-harm".
How many people in Britain experience mental health
problems? The Office for National Statistics or ONS puts
the figure at one in six adults at any one
time. Another major survey that is frequently quoted puts

the figure at one in four.

Depression and mood disorders are now common illnesses in our society with as many as 30% of the adult population suffering depression at some stage in their life.

Treating someone with depression should examine various aspects of their life including nutrition, relationships, exercise regime, sleep patterns and relaxation.

Having worked extensively with people suffering from depression it is clear that using affirmations alongside visualizations, good nutrition and exercise can dramatically ease the symptoms of depression and often eliminate depression entirely.

The kind of internal dialogue we have with ourselves is very important to our overall mental health. Most people are not even aware of their negative mental dialogue as it becomes a habit. We need to be taught awareness of our thoughts before we can actually change them.

I have noticed that people who suffer from depression usually have very negative self-talk and this needs to be worked at and changed in order to increase one's self esteem and allow a person to begin making a recovery.

The saying "As you think, you become" is very true.

Our thoughts create our future. Many people who suffer depression have persistent negative thoughts for a majority of the time, sometimes from when they waken up in the morning until they go to bed. If we think negative thoughts often enough they will become our belief. It has been proven that our thoughts affect us at a cellular level and continuous negative thoughts have a detrimental effect on the cell structure which can leave us with a weakened immune system and more susceptible to disease.

One of the most effective tools in treating depression is through using affirmations.

Affirmations are positive phrases that are to be repeated as many times as possible throughout the day. They work by replacing negative thoughts logged in the subconscious mind with positive, nurturing thoughts. It is impossible to have negative thoughts at the same time as positive thoughts.

Our subconscious mind believes what it is told and if it is fed positive messages it will eventually believe them.

Positive words or thoughts have a huge impact on how we feel and our feelings affects our behavior and therefore, what we do or don't take on in life.

The best results come from those who are open minded and willing to put in the work doing the affirmations on a daily basis.

Affirmations have to be present tense, positive and personal.

Saying these affirmations may feel strange, even silly at first but after a while they won't feel this way and the subconscious mind will begin through repetition to believe what it is being told. Don't give up!

Examples of affirmations to help with depression are:

I am at one with myself

I love and approve of myself exactly as I am

I am calm and relaxed

I handle whatever happens

I am confident, assertive and decisive in every situation

My body and mind are healthy

I am full of energy and enthusiasm

When we repeat these affirmations over and over again the subconscious mind believes these messages and tries to make it our reality. I have noticed that when a depressed person is really working with affirmations they are able to make some really big positive changes in their life. Some of my students have been able to return to work or college because the depression has lifted and they have a new, fresher more positive outlook on life. They handle stress and upsets better. They find that they handle relationships better and life in general is much improved.

Affirmations are a fantastic tool to aid recovery and it is understated how effective they are in alleviating depression. When we are repeating positive affirmations daily we begin to feel better about ourselves which in turn boosts our self-esteem. Affirmations can be practiced any time of the day. Before you get out of bed in the morning repeat your affirmations. This is a good start to the day. The key to long lasting change is daily repetition of affirmations. You will soon notice the difference in your mood.

The following are some questions to ask when we are feeling depressed. Take a piece of paper and take some time to answer these questions honestly and from the heart.

Am I confusing a thought with a fact?

What evidence do I have to support what I think about myself?

Are these self-critical thoughts helpful to me?

Am I using a double standard?

Am I expecting myself to be perfect?

Am I condemning myself on the basis of one single event?

Am I concentrating on my weaknesses and ignoring my strengths?"

End of article.

Ways to help with depression

Laughter and happiness produce endorphins to make the body feel good. Even just smiling releases serotonin, a happy neurotransmitter into the bloodstream and acts as a powerful antidepressant. Watch funny movies!

Take physical exercise as it helps use up the adrenaline that has been released into the bloodstream as a result of stress. Exercise produces natural opiates in the body which makes you feel good for hours afterwards.

Acknowledge when you are having negative thoughts and decide to change your thoughts. Each time you do, it strengthens the neural pathways in the brain that are associated with pleasure and reinforces the happy chemicals in the body.

We must put our goals into action. Every day if we

take a step or some steps however small they may be towards our goal, it will become easier and then we will see that taking action becomes our new good habit.

'Truly successful people take action before they are ready'. Don't learn to accept your perceived limitations. It is said that 'learned helplessness' is one of the key causes of depression, inaction and self-defeating behavior.

Heal your body, use your mind.

"You'll see it when you believe it." This is the title of a great book by Dr. Wayne Dyer. It is so true and yet often so many people will only believe something when they can actually see it. Science has now proven that when we believe in something either positive or indeed negative the sub-conscious mind goes to work on giving us what we asked for, so be careful what you ask for you might just get it! We have the power to heal our bodies by using visualization techniques combined with positive affirmations.

We know that our emotions are linked to the cells in our body. When we feel embarrassed for example our face goes red. When we watch a sad movie this can activate the tear ducts to produce tears. When we hear or see something that frightens us the hairs on our arms stand up. When we feel nervous before an event our palms may sweat and our heart beat increases. All these physical symptoms happen because of changes in our emotions.

I have had psoriasis for over 20 years. It began as a tiny patch on my left upper thigh and has gradually spread to most of both legs. The psoriasis was mainly confined to my legs until October 2008 when I was going through an emotionally difficult period it began to form new patches on my arms, hand and neck. This caused me great distress as it was extremely itchy and I could only wear cotton next to my skin.

In February 2009 I attended a seminar by Dr. David Hamilton (see Chapter 1) on the power of our minds to heal our body. I started doing some visualization work twice daily and can now report one month later the patches on my arms, hands and neck have cleared. I attribute this totally to the visualization work I have been doing.

Here is the visualization I used. Try it before you get out of bed in the morning and before going to sleep. It can be adapted to suit you.

Close your eyes and visualize yourself going into your body's cells, you can see the psoriasis cells; they are red and irritated looking. Thank them for being there but tell them it is time for them to leave your body.

Now starting at the top of your body visualize yourself again inside your body and you are holding a magnet. As you slowly move all the way down through your body the magnet is attracting all the psoriasis cells. If the magnet gets too full you can introduce a new magnet to pick up where you left. Do this until all the psoriasis cells have gone. Now see them leave through the soles of your feet and deposited into Mother Earth.

Now starting at the crown visualize a ray of white light spreading slowly through your entire body, cleansing it as it moves all through the body parts. See in your mind's eye how beautiful your skin is now, completely clear of any psoriasis. See yourself doing something that you didn't do before because of the psoriasis. I visualize myself in a swimsuit just about to enter a pool on a lovely sunny day. I am smiling and I feel totally comfortable and confident in myself. I love my new body. After I have completed the visualization I repeat the following affirmation,

"The healing process has begun."'

I am now aware that I created the conditions for my psoriasis to spread through my negative thoughts and feelings. The good news is I now have the power to change my thoughts and clear my psoriasis. This is exciting and liberating for me.

The Power of Affirmations.

An affirmation is a statement repeated over and over again either verbally or mentally. They are positive, present tense; personal statements that will help you change those negative beliefs that may be holding you back from being the best you can be.

Affirmations change the way you think and feel about things, and because you have replaced dysfunctional beliefs with your own new positive beliefs, positive change comes easily and naturally.

The idea behind affirmations is to replace the negative thoughts with new positive, powerful, self-nurturing ones. By using and repeating these powerful affirmations you can retrain your mind to think and feel differently about any given situation.

Affirmations become more powerful when spoken, thought or written with a strong 'feeling' attached. Visualizing what it will be like when you have boundless confidence in every area of your life will reinforce the message to the subconscious mind.

How quickly the affirmations work depends on how much resistance you have with an affirmation and this relates to how deeply the belief is held and how determined you are to bring about positive changes in your life.

Positive thinking and health.

Can the way we think and the thoughts we think affect our health?

Research has shown that positive people enjoy better health, have fewer days off work and enjoy life more.

Positive thinking however doesn't come naturally to everyone. I personally have to work very hard at it, but with practice it becomes easier. I learn to catch myself sooner when I am speaking negatively or if myself talk is negative. In order to become a more positive person you have to first become aware of your thoughts, become a 'thought patroller, constantly monitoring our thoughts. Most people have 90% the same thoughts today as they did yesterday and negative thinking can become habitual.

When we procrastinate we do ourselves a great injustice. Often negative thoughts we have about ourselves are just not true and stem from a feeling of

'I'm not good enough' or 'I don't deserve' mentality. We ought to ask ourselves 'Who am I not good enough for?' and 'Why do I think I am undeserving of something?' We are our own worst critics. If you had a friend who spoke to you the way you sometimes speak to yourself, you probably wouldn't stay friends with that person for very long, yet this is what we do to ourselves daily.

When we have a good balance in our life between, work, family and enjoyment we are much more likely to find it easier to feel positive. It is therefore very important to work at maintaining all the elements that make up our life. Maybe we need to address certain aspects that are out of balance and give time to making positive changes. It will be time well spent. There are some simple things we can do to help us on our way to becoming a more positive person.

The practice of Gratitude.

Recall at least five things every day that made you smile or gave you a warm, happy feeling. These can be very simple things for example, someone paying you a compliment, hearing birds singing in your garden. Going for a walk is the easiest way to feel gratitude because there is beauty all around us, we just have to open our eyes and notice. When we are in a state of gratitude we cannot have negative thoughts simultaneously. The more often you are noticing things to be grateful for the less time you will have to think negative thought. Try it and notice how your mood improves. This is a really good habit to get into. I like to record mine in my gratitude journal.

Complain Less.

I bought a 'Complaint free' bracelet (see Chapter 1) to help monitor how many times I complain about something or someone. The idea behind it is that every time you complain, gossip or criticize you transfer the band from one wrist to the other and in so

doing you can monitor any 'complaining words'.

Scientists believe it takes 21 days to form a new habit

and complaining is habitual for most of us. The task

is to be able to reach the 21 days without

complaining, gossiping of criticizing. This may take

you several months to achieve as each time, you

complain etc. you have to start all over again! These

purple bands can be purchased at

www.AComplaintFreeWorld.org. They are a powerful

tool to remind ourselves that we create our future with

the thoughts we have.

Positive affirmations.

These will replace negative thoughts we might harbor.

They must be personal, present tense and positive.

Examples of positive affirmations for health could be:

I lovingly take care of my body and it takes care of me

The healing process has already begun

My body feels balanced and in perfect harmony

I am filled with energy and vitality

Say these affirmations as often as you can. Say them with meaning. Even if you don't believe them the subconscious mind will start to believe them if repeated often enough. It will then try and make the statements you have been feeding it, your reality. I suggest writing them out and sticking them around the house until affirmations become a new habit for you.

The more often you say the affirmations and the more emotion you can attach whilst saying them the faster you will see results.

Reduce stressors.

You might say, easier said than done! However, by taking a little time to assess exactly what it is that causes stress in our life will allow you to make changes for the better. Maybe being more organized will help reduce a cluttered environment. De cluttering your home step by step can be like a weight off your shoulders. It is a great exercise to do as your mind too will feel lighter and calmer.

Do activities that you enjoy.

What kind of things do you enjoy doing best? Plan how you can do the things you enjoy and incorporate it into your daily routine. Do one thing you enjoy every day, just for you and DO NOT feel guilty as this completely defeats the purpose. Doing something that you enjoy will make you feel better and you will learn to value and appreciate yourself more.

Have a laugh.

There's nothing better than having a good hearty laugh. It is great for your health. When was the last time you had a good laugh? It's quite contagious!

Take time to relax and unwind.

Try and build in some relaxation time every day. This might only be 15 minutes but it will be 15 minutes of quality relaxation time. Run a nice bath for yourself, add some of your favorite oils and light some candles. Get used to pampering yourself a little. Your worth it and let no-one tell you different!

Put things in perspective.

Whenever you feel down try and remember those who are worse off. If you are complaining that it is raining. Remind yourself how lucky you are to be sheltered from the rain in your warm car and how lucky you are that you have a house to live in and that you are not homeless, sleeping rough at night. Then you realize just how lucky you really are.

Get plenty of rest.

Good quality sleep is very important for our mental health and overall wellbeing. Life can look a whole lot different after a good night sleep. We cope better with life's stresses after restful sleep.

Eat a healthy diet.

It goes without saying that we should eat a healthy well balanced diet. We are what we eat! By eating healthily, we are ensuring that our body is been fed all the nutrients it requires to function efficiently. You will have increased energy, sleep better and look better generally. When you look and feel healthy it is easier to be more positive about life.

Exercise every day.

Thirty minutes every day will make an amazing difference not only to your physical shape and fitness levels but also to your mental state. Feel good endorphins are released into the blood stream when you exercise. Choose a form of exercise that you enjoy doing as you are more likely to stick to it.

Relaxation Exercise

Get yourself into a comfortable seated position with your feet on the floor, palms resting on your lap facing upward.

Close your eyes and imagine you are lying on the shoreline of a long golden beach. You are lying with your feet towards the water and your head relaxing on the fine, smooth sand.

As you are lying there, feel the golden sun beaming down on your body. It is the perfect temperature right now.

Gaze towards the light and imagine the sun's rays connecting between your center and the center of the ball of warmth and light.

Feel how the sun beats down and warms your every cell. The light is powerful and refreshing and it is flooding through your body.

Your breathing is deep and slow. Now you begin to feel the water brush up and under your body as it lays on the sand.

The first little wave of water just touches your toes and the backs of your legs. As it returns to the sea it softens the sand below your body.

The next wave sends water under your body and up to your waist. Your body sinks into the sand as, once again; the water flows back into the sea taking with it any tension or stress. Just feel it wash away.

The next wave comes up and under your shoulders and gently cools your neck. As it flows back towards the sea it takes all the tension away.

The next wave travels beneath your head. You feel your head sink into the sand and your hair rinsed by the warm water.

Now you can focus on your whole body. You are cleansed and free of tension. The light is still focused on your center and your body can take as much as it wishes. You can drink it until your body feels drenched in golden light, inside and out.

Now move your eyes to the sky and see the last drops of light drain into your body. The beam now leaves the sun and is absorbed into your body. Start to move your hands and feet slowly. You are now full of light, energized, refreshed. Your body is nourished and you feel wonderful.

Seven Ways to become more calm!

1. Take 5 long, slow breaths, breathing in through the nose and out through the mouth. Abdominal breathing or belly breathing calms the sympathetic nervous system and allows us to think with more clarity. If we can get in the habit if doing deep breathing before we step out of bed in the morning and last thing at night, or when you are sitting at the traffic lights or working at your desk you will feel tremendous benefits in a short space of time.

2. Take a few minutes to yourself just to be quiet and try and look at the big picture. Sometimes when we are all caught up in our worries or problems we can't 'see the wood for the trees'. Take a few deep breaths and ask a higher power than you, God, the Universe to guide you through this period in your life and give you

direction.

3. Count your blessing every day. Count all the
   little things in your life for which you are
   grateful. Try and write down or acknowledge 5
   things you are grateful for each day. When we
   are focused on what we do have we cannot be
   thinking about the lack in our life. Put things in
   perspective.

4. We don't always have to agree with everyone
   else opinion. It's okay to disagree as long as it
   is done in a respectful manner where yours
   and other people's self-esteem remains intact.

5. Live in the here and now, be present and
   mindful of what you are doing. Try not let our
   mind go here and there it will become very
   tiring. When for example doing the dishes, be
   present, be aware of the sensation of water, try

and focus on the job you are doing. It is in a sense a type of meditation as you are trying to focus the mind on one task at a time instead of it being scattered all over the place.

6. Try and identify your stressors and find out what you do to minimize them. When we feel stressed or anxious we cannot feel calm and relaxed so here is a good time to use the affirmations:

'I am calm and relaxed, I am at peace'.

7. Let go of attachment to the past. Remember the saying 'yesterday is history, tomorrow a mystery, today is a gift that's why they call it the present.'

Here is a summary of tips for becoming a more positive person, healthy in body and mind.

Practice gratitude.

Every night, recall 3-5 things that you are grateful for or appreciated during that day.

Complain less.

Try wearing a 'complaint free' band

Practice daily affirmations and visualization.

Practice relaxation techniques and deep breathing.

Reduce stressors – write down what your stressors are and how you can eliminate or reduce them.

Exercise daily, do some form you enjoy and will maintain.

Eat regular and nutritious food.

Get plenty of sleep.

Have a laugh, read or watch something funny.

Take time to relax and unwind.

Put things in perspective.

Journal your thoughts and feelings, the good and the bad.

Spend time with friends and family.

Talk to someone you trust about a problem or situation.

Do something just for you every day, even if it's something small.

Take on a new challenge that excites you.

Chapter Ten

Limiting Beliefs

"Nothing binds you except your thoughts, nothing

limits you except your fear and nothing controls you

except your beliefs."

Marianne Williamson

Limiting beliefs can stop you from accomplishing all the wonderful things you want to do in life.

Sometimes we are not even aware we have limiting beliefs.

Some questions to ask yourself.

What are my beliefs about money?

What was I taught about money whilst growing up?

Was money the 'route of all evil'?

Were we told 'money doesn't grow on trees'?

If we have thoughts that we do not have enough and our focus remains on our 'lack of' we will attract more of that into our life and be able to manifest a good income because our limiting belief about money will prevent us attracting it into our life. We need to be able to believe that money can be a good thing for us and can be used for good. We need to believe there is enough for everyone and we too are deserving of money.

If we have a limiting belief about deserving money, this will be stored in your subconscious mind and it will sabotage any opportunity for you to attract money into your life.

Some affirmations I like to use here are:

'I attract abundance and prosperity into my life',

'Abundance and prosperity flow my way'

Practice these often if you need to have more money in your life and you will be amazed at what the Universe will send your way!

We can harbor limiting beliefs about other things such as love, career, men, women, sex. The main limiting belief I have come across in working with clients over the years is 'deserving.' The limiting belief that 'I don't deserve that' can prevent the flow of what we really want from showing up in our life. I don't deserve to be happy, to have loving relationships, to have financial freedom, to have a lovely home, to have that job and the list goes on. Feeling that we don't deserve stems from a feeling of 'I am not worth it' 'I am not good enough'. To change these feelings which are not making us feel good about ourselves we need to learn to love ourselves exactly as we are.

An affirmation to help us feel more loving towards ourselves is:

'I love and approve of myself exactly as I am'

If we can look ourselves in the mirror every day and say these words we may initially feel strange about what we see in the mirror but over time we will learn to love the person we are looking at in the mirror. We are doing the best we can, so be gentle with yourself.

We need to examine our beliefs because our main beliefs systems were already established by the age of 5 and so the beliefs we had then may not hold true as the adult we are now. For example, we may have been told as a child to never talk to strangers. This would have been good advice from our parents at the time and helped us keep safe. However, at age 35 the idea of not talking to strangers does not fit or serve us any longer, so we need to examine our beliefs and ask ourselves, ' is this belief true for me now at this stage in my life?'.

If we continue to believe something that is not true about ourselves, others or the world this can stop you from being the wonderful person you are supposed to be and prevent us reaching our true, real potential in life.

Fear has two meanings – Forget everything and Run!

Or Face everything and Rise! The choice is yours.

FEAR can be viewed as False Evidence Appearing

Real!

The limitations we have placed upon ourselves

manifest themselves in the form of pain, unhappiness

and dis-ease. We need to take stock, be quiet and

find inner peace before we can address these

blockages or limitations. Then and only then can

healing begin. It has been shown that during

meditation and relaxation our resistance to disease is

increased.

I like the phrase from The Matte Bhava Meditation

(Loving Kindness Meditation)

'May I be well, may I be happy, may all things go well

for me'.

Changing Patterns of behavior

'If you don't set a baseline standard for what you'll accept in your life, you'll find it's easy to slip into behaviors and attitudes or a quality of life that's far below what you deserve.'

Tony Robbins

Whatever we link pain and pleasure to will shape our destiny. As human beings we are not so much driven by what we know from an intellectual perspective but rather by what we have learned to associate pain and pleasure to in our nervous system. It is this neuro-association of pain and pleasure that will determine our actions. Therefore, if we are to make lasting change, we need to associate pain with our old behavior and pleasure with the new behavior. It is not the events in our life that shape us but the meaning we give to these events. All our personal breakthroughs begin with changing our belief first. When we can switch the belief linking any negative behavior to feelings of pain we can then make lasting changes.

We have to decide what changes we want to make in our life and what level of commitment we are prepared to go to in order to achieve our new goals. Every new goal we set for ourselves must be matched with taking action otherwise it will never come to fruition.

I attended Unity Church Houston on Sunday October 7, 2012 and Reverend Michael Gott's talk that day was truly inspirational.

"Use what talent you possess: the woods would be very silent if no birds sang except those that sang the best".

Henry Van Dyke

Rev. Gott talked about increasing our faith. Sometimes we need to take a leap of faith so we can become evolved in our spiritual growth. Our faith will allow us to move forward in our life. There are some common qualities found in the greatest leaders of our time. They live at the level of cause not effect. They live in the domain of faith and faith-based people are people of growth and expansion. People of faith are people who take action. If we do nothing, nothing will change! If we just trust and 'let go' of what is holding us back the universe will help us. We have to be courageous enough to take the next step knowing we have the power within to do this. We have to take action, as God can only do for us what God can do through you.

Self-Esteem

One's self-esteem will determine the results of whatever we undertake. It can work for us or be our own worst enemy. If you think you deserve something and yourself-esteem is also high, yourself esteem will subconsciously help you achieve what you want by guiding you to make the necessary decisions to get it. The opposite of course is also true.

How do we improve our self-esteem?

We can improve our self-esteem by doing things that make us feel good about ourselves. Also when other people say good things to us or about us it helps boost our self-esteem. Try thinking good thoughts about ourselves and try to be less critical is a good start. Studies show that 86% of what we say to ourselves is negative, so we need to pay more attention to our self-talk and catch ourselves when we are being harsh or critical. There is a direct relationship between self-esteem and success. It is a virtuous cycle; the more success we achieve no matter how small the higher our self-esteem becomes. If our self-esteem is low we need to ask ourselves:

'What is holding me back from achieving the success I say I want?

Is fear holding you back?

Is fear of success preventing you from succeeding or fear of failure, rejection?

We need to take responsibility for where we are in our life and how we arrived at this point. Don't be a victim, do not blame others. Take control of your life and how you react to life's events. We do not always have control over circumstances or people but what we do have control over is how we react and recover from life's hardships and knocks. Believe in yourself, belief you have the power and strength within to handle whatever comes your way.

'I handle everything that comes my way with ease.'

Patricia.

Patricia came to see me as her sadness after her boyfriend broke up with her was affecting her training and she had a triathlon race coming up. Even though her boyfriend of a year was not very loving or kind to her she would rather be with him than be alone.

Her self-esteem was low and her self-talk was negating and self-critical.

She felt desperate and wanted nothing more than to share her life with a loving man. We worked on her self-worth and Law of Attraction to bring the right person into her life. She had to learn to leave the past behind and create the life she knew she deserved. You have to make room for the universe to bring you what you want but Patricia still pined for her ex-boyfriend and in so doing was not allowing the universe to bring her Mr. Right.

We worked on the following affirmations:

'I attract loving relationships into my life'.

'I am worthy and deserving of all things good'.

'I am a strong and confident woman'.

'I release and let go of any person, place or thing that no longer serves me'.

She reported that after a while of practicing these affirmations her energy improved and her confidence in herself came back allowing her to return to full training. She felt hopeful of now being able to attract a loving partner into her life.

John.

John came to see me feeling he had lost his passion for life and couldn't find his purpose.

He had been chosen to be one of six athletes to represent his country in rowing in the 1996 Olympics. He had done all the hard training and travelled to the Olympic camp hoping he would be one of the four chosen to be in the boat. He was not chosen. He watched his team mates receive their silver medals on the podium. He got a T-shirt! He explained that with other Olympic sports all athletes who are in the Olympic camp receive a medal if their team win even if they were not chosen to compete, but this was not the case for rowing. Although he was very pleased for his team mates he felt disappointed he was not part of the race.

He described himself as 'having a chip on his shoulder' still and did not feel he was good enough, even though this was 20 years on from the event. His self-esteem was very low having had to give up his job and move to Houston as his wife took a promotion with her company. John decided to take up triathlon but only if he could reach his goal and be number one in the world. Nothing short of this would be acceptable to him. His training had come to halt as he developed pain in his right shoulder, right elbow and right knee. The right side of the body relates to the feminine side so I asked him what type of relationship he had with his mother. His mother had passed away some years back and suffered with bipolar disease which manifested in severe bouts of mania followed by periods of depression because she would not take her medication. At the age of 8 he had overheard a conversation between his parents where his mother said there would be no point paying for private education for John as he was not clever and it would be a waste of money. So this child grew up with low self-esteem and lacking in confidence. There was very little affection shown to him of his sister from either parents. John was a highly intelligent man but still had very low self-esteem and although he was super fit and lean he had body issues and saw himself as fat.

John came to see me over the space of two months and we worked on deserving, forgiveness, reprogramming the subconscious mind with positive affirmations, gratitude. There was a lot of resistance to change even though he agreed he would be a happier person by making some changes to his negative thinking patterns. We worked hard to boost his self-esteem and confidence levels.

Affirmations for Self Esteem

I am totally adequate for all situations

I choose to feel good about myself. I am worthy of my own love.

I stand on my own two feet. I accept and use my own power.

It is safe for me to speak up for myself.

It does not matter what other people say or do. What matters is how I choose to react to believe about myself.

I take a deep breath and allow myself to relax. My entire body calms down.

I am loved and accepted exactly as I am, right here

and right now.

I see the world through eyes of love and acceptance.

All is well in my world.

My self-esteem is high because I honor who I am.

I accept others as they are; and they, in turn, accept

me.

I am wonderful, and I feel great. I am grateful for my

life.

This is the only time I get to live today. I choose to

enjoy it.

I have the self-esteem, power, and confidence to

move forward in life with ease.

The greatest gift I can give myself is unconditional

love.

I love myself exactly as I am. I no longer wait to be perfect in order to love myself.

Chapter Eleven

How to thrive under the Global Pandemic of 2020

"Life isn't about waiting for the storm to pass. It's about learning to dance in the rain.

Susan Ryan

I felt the book would not be complete without talking about the Coronavirus health pandemic that is sweeping the world and causing so much death through the disease it causes, Covid-19. At the time of writing, May 2, 2020 there have been over a 3,500,000 cases of Covid-19 and 250,000 recorded deaths worldwide. These numbers will likely increase as the pandemic takes hold.

The pandemic has caused widespread fear, anxiety and stress for a lot of people. There is fear over jobs losses, fear of catching the virus or our elderly or sick loved ones becoming ill. Businesses have taken a hit and the economy has crashed. Nobody has been unaffected by the virus as lockdowns and social distancing has become the 'norm' all over the world. Amongst all the fear and sadness that surrounds us at this time there are things we can do to help ourselves stay safe and healthy. We have been protecting ourselves physically by washing hands for the recommended 20 seconds with soap and water, self-isolating and not being in contact with anyone outside immediate family members. Wearing masks when entering the supermarket and extra precautions when cleaning surfaces are among new measures in the hope of slowing down the virus. There have been some good lessons to be learned from other countries and many things we wish were done differently for sure.

Most countries have seen environmental benefits as a result of Coronavirus.

Researchers around the world have seen a drop in air pollutants as a result of fewer cars on the road and exhaust from factories.

Satellite photos of China show an unprecedented drop in pollution. Worldwide greenhouse gas emissions are falling.

Our planet has benefited from the couple of months where there have been restrictions on air traffic, fewer vehicles on the roads, fewer ships on our ocean.

What I noticed during this time where children are been home schooled and parents are at home either because they have lost jobs or are working from home is that families seem to be spending more time together. The nearby trails where I live have been busier with children on bikes and scooters, people jogging and walking. It has been lovely to see families out in nature more than ever. We can hear the birds singing in the trees happily, the grass looks greener and there is a sense the planet is saying 'thank you' for giving us a rest from the loudness, pollution, busyness and bustling that has sadly become our norm. There is a wonderful quietness on the roads, in our skies and all over the world as nature gets a chance to revive a little.

Here are some ideas to help ease stress at this time. If you are reading this book and the Coronavirus is a thing of the past, great! However, use the tips for the next thing that may come along to disrupt our world whether that is on a personal or global level.

We have been bombarded by the media with constant news about the Coronavirus and although I feel it is important to keep abreast of what is going on in the world it is also important to not view the TV news channels constantly as it can easily put us into a state of being overwhelmed.

What my family is focused on during this difficult and unprecedented time in our lifetime is keeping our immune system strong. As 70% of our immune system is housed in our gut it is imperative that we keep our digestive system in really good working order. We can do this of course by having a healthy diet, taking probiotics and pre-biotics to feed the good bacteria and maintain a healthy gut flora. However, it is essential for us to manage our stress levels at this difficult time in our life because unmanaged stress is our biggest killer. Stress damages our immune system and makes us more susceptible to disease. So we need to be in great shape mentally and physically to stay healthy in the midst of this pandemic. Even if we do contract the virus when we are healthy, we will have a much stronger chance of overcoming its harmful effects. You can read more about managing stress in my book '10 ways to reduce and manage stress'.

Although there is much fear, uncertainty, stress and sadness that surrounds this global pandemic it is important that we are accepting of the changes that have been forced upon us and become adaptable to a new way of life.

We can stay positive, be grateful every day for all our big and little blessings and use our mind to stay not in a place of fear but in a place of hope. It is crucial we stay healthy in our mind and body now more than ever. Practice deep abdominal breathing, exercise, eat well, rest, relax, stay in contact with family and friends through our smart devices, mend broken relationships. Value what is important in life and maintain perspective. Let the little things go that are really not that important. Use the quiet, isolation to learn a new skill, hobby, finish a book (which is exactly what I'm doing!), deepen your spiritual practices by practicing gratitude every day for all you have, meditate, read uplifting material, laugh more, pray more, talk to family and friends more.

Surely this Coronavirus pandemic must make us wake up to the fact that we are all One people, living on One planet and we are all connected. Surely it must make us see that we as humans have more in common than we do not. The virus does not discriminate between the color of our skin, nor our religious or political beliefs, nor the amount of wealth we have acquired. The virus doesn't care about any of this and nor should we. We need to wake up, smell the roses and realize we are all in this crisis together and if we unite, we will conquer it. If we do not, well that's another matter. I do not know what state our planet will be in at the time you will be reading this book, hopefully it will be in better shape! My wish is that we come through this pandemic learning lessons that are important. We only have one planet and we can make it a better place for us to live on, not only for us but for future generations to come. This is our wakeup call! This is our call to action for the world to unite and make our beautiful a better place for all to live.

Finding our authentic Self

The word 'authentic' comes from the Latin word 'authenticus' and Greek word, 'authentikos' meaning principal or genuine. This is our true nature and where we find peace. The mind as we all know can take us into places that are not healthy. It can take us to places of being upset or angry, places that are not the 'true self'. When we do not stand up for ourselves and speak our truth we do ourselves a great disservice. 'What keeps us from growing and expanding?' Much of the time the answer to this question is 'fear'. Fear of success, fear of failure, fear of rejection. One of the greatest challenges on our spiritual path is to find out who we are. The real you are a creation of God or if you prefer 'love'. Our spiritual evolution is about looking at the parts of us that we may not like, owning these parts and committing to cleansing these parts of ourselves that are less than whole. These parts I'm referring to could be jealousy, envy, hatred, unkindness or any negative characteristic that is not our true essence. There is inner conflict when we are not honoring our authentic self and if we take a closer look at when that happens, usually the ego will be involved.

Our journey on this planet involves us revealing who we truly are and committing daily to being our authentic self, our true nature and being the best possible version of ourselves. We are all on different paths to the one destination. Be kind, compassionate and loving to yourself. The heart knows the way home.

Bibliography

The Breakthrough Experience, Dr. John F Demartini

Law of Attraction, Dr. David Hamilton

A primer in Positive Psychology, Christopher Petersen

Medicine and Miracles, Bernie Siegel

The Secret, Rhonda Byrne

Healing mind, healing body, Debbie Shapiro

Healing into Life and Death, Stephen Levine

Power of the Soul, John Holland

When the Body Says No, Dr. Gabor Maté

About the Author

Miriam Mills lives in Houston, Texas with her husband

Alan, daughter Niamh and their adorable dog 'Dylan'.

She is the founder of Breathe Flow Balance and the

author of '10 Ways to Reduce and Manage Stress'.

She is a Life Coach, Stress Management Consultant,

speaker and workshop Facilitator.

Visit www.breatheflowbalance.com

www.ingramcontent.com/pod-product-compliance
Lightning Source LLC
Chambersburg PA
CBHW051423150726
48000CB00005B/1932